MW01443187

Running Tap Journal

Blank 200 page journal

DiBiasio Publications

Cover design by Brendon DiBiasio

Made in United States
Orlando, FL
06 January 2024

42193548R00114